For Tope & Olaolu

Sikulu and Harambe by the Zambezi River
An African version of the Good Samaritan Story

Blue Brush Media
Renton, WA
www.bluebrushmedia.com

Design by Abacus Graphics, Oceanside, CA – abacusgraphics.com

Library of Congress Control Number: 2008901414

ISBN-13:978-0-9777382-4-3
ISBN-10:0-9777382-4-8

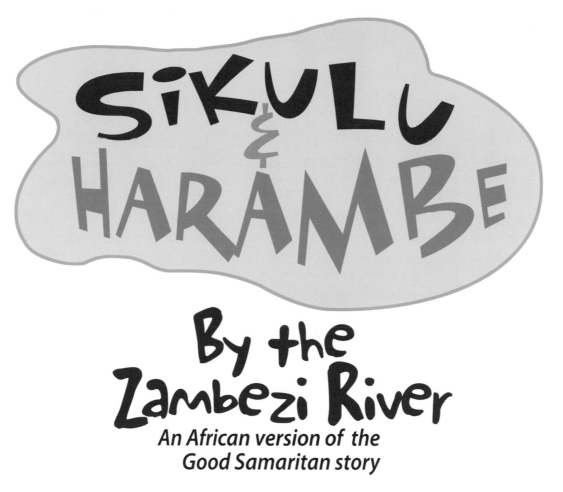

SIKULU & HARAMBE

By the Zambezi River

*An African version of the
Good Samaritan story*

Kunle Oguneye
Illustrations by Bruce McCorkindale

One afternoon, in the village of Sioma, **Sikulu** (*sea coo lu*) the spider and **Harambe** (*Ha ram bay*) the hippo were playing hide and seek.

"I'm thirsty!" said Harambe. "Hop on. Let's go down to the river."

Mundia (*moon dee a*) the elephant and Imasiku (E *ma see coo*) the stork were already at the river, just as Lubinda (L*oo bin da*) the river fish and her friends were swimming upstream to find their lunch.

Far in the distance, Sikulu saw an old woman washing her clothes.

Suddenly the old woman slipped. "Help!" cried the old woman, "my clothes will be lost to the river. Somebody, please help me!"

"**W**e will help you," yelled Sikulu.
"Come Harambe, let's help the old woman."

They ran to help the old woman, but they were very far away and she could not hear them. She ran along the riverbank following her clothes and crying out, "Help me!"

Lubinda and her friends were closer. Perhaps the river fish would help the old woman. "River fish, friends of the Zambezi," said the old woman, "please save my clothes. I am too old to swim."

"We're sorry," Lubinda said.
"We're swimming upstream and
your clothes are floating downstream.
We cannot help you." They
flicked their tails and swam away.

Imasiku was looking for lunch on the riverbank. Perhaps he would help the old woman. "Dear stork, friend of the Zambezi," said the old woman, "please save my clothes. I am too old to swim."

"*I*'m sorry,"
Imasiku the stork said.
"I am looking for my lunch.
I cannot help you."
Then he waded deeper into the water.

Mundia was
drinking water at
the riverbank. Perhaps
Mundia would help the
old woman, reasoned
Sikulu. "Great elephant,
friend of the Zambezi,"
said the old woman,
"please save my clothes.
I am too old to swim."

"**I**'m sorry,"
Mundia the elephant said.
"Today is not my bath day
and I do not wish to get wet."
Then he dipped his very long trunk
back into the river and began drinking.

"Don't worry, mama," called Harambe. "We'll help you save your clothes!" yelled Sikulu. Sikulu was scared because he could not swim, but he clung courageously to Harambe's ears as the two friends went into the water.

"Watch out!" Harambe yelled as Sikulu was almost washed away by a big splash.

Sikulu and Harambe struggled against the strong river currents to save the old woman's clothes.

"Thank you, my children" said the old woman. "It was very kind of you to help someone you don't know. As a reward for your kindness, please dip your hands into this pot and take whatever you find."

Sikulu dipped his long spidery legs
into the pot. "Bati!" he exclaimed.
When he pulled them out they
had glistening emerald and
gold bracelets on them.

"Bati!" exclaimed Harambe
when he dipped his legs into the pot and
pulled out a beautiful *chitenge* cloth fit for kings.

"These are beautiful," said Harambe and Sikulu, "but we do not deserve such valuable gifts." "Oh yes you do, my children!" said the old woman. "Any kindness is its own reward. But, Sikulu, you faced your fear of the water to help someone in need, and you, Harambe, helped him overcome his fear."

It just so happened that the following Saturday was the "Ku-omboka" ceremony. It was the biggest event of the year for the Lozi peple. Everyone was dressed in his or her best. Sikulu wore the gold and emerald braclets, and Harambe wore his brightly colored *chitenge*.

"What beautiful bracelets!" said Lubinda the river fish. "You look like a prince." "What a gorgeous chitenge!" said Imasiku the stork. "You look like a king."

"**W**here did you find them?" asked Mundia the elephant. All three were filled with envy for Sikulu and Harambe.

"**W**e got them from
the old woman at the river,"
said Harambe. "Which old woman
was that?" asked Lubinda. "The old woman
who was washing her clothes," replied Sikulu.
"It was a reward for helping her save her clothes."

Lubinda, Imasiku, and Mundia remembered refusing to help the old woman and felt very ashamed. They wished that they had helped the old woman, and decided they would behave differently the next time someone needed their help.

What is the moral of the story?

Can you remember a time when you needed help and no one helped you?

Can you remember a time when someone needed help and you didn't help that person?

Share your responses and read other people's responses on sikulu.com
(Please get your parent's permission before sharing your responses on the website).

Glossary of words, names, and places:

Sikulu = is a South African name that belonged to a great warrior

Harambe = is a Swahili word that means "let's come together as one."

Bati = is an expression of surprise similar to "wow"

Eshula! = means to overcome or to win in Lozi language.

Chitenge = Chitenge cloth is native to Zambia. Chitenge holds a special place in the heart of Zambians. Newborn babies are wrapped in a chitenge as soon as they are delivered.

Lozi people = are from western Zambia. Lozi are also found in Namibia, Angola and Botswana.

Zambezi River = is the fourth-longest river in Africa. It starts in Zambia and flows through three other African countries before it empties into the Indian Ocean.

Victoria Falls = The Zambezi river tumbles 420 feet (128 metres) into a narrow valley. Its original name is the Mosi-oa-Tunya, "the smoke that thunders." It is twice the height of Niagara Falls.

Ku-omboka Ceremony

The Ku-omboka Ceremony is the most important Lozi festival. It has taken place for over 300 years. Ku-omboka means to get out of the water onto dry land. The Lozi people live close to the Zambezi River. During the rainy season, their homes are flooded and they have to move to higher ground, where it's safer.

The Litunga or Chief decides when it is time to leave, usually in February or March. The royal drums are sounded and the Lozi people pack their belongings into canoes.

The procession to higher ground is led by the *Litunga* and his wife, the *Moyo*, each in their own royal barge. The procession takes several hours to reach the forest region where the celebration continues.

Elephant: The elephant is the largest land animal. They are very good swimmers and have been known to swim nonstop for up to 6 miles. They spend up to 18 hours a day feeding. Elephants weigh as much as 12 full-size pick up trucks.

Spider: Spiders have eight legs and feed on insects. They have between two and eight eyes. Spiders are not insects and they can't fly. There are over 10,000 different species of spiders in the world.

Hippopotamus: Hippos spend most of the day resting in the water. They don't like the heat so they have to remain cool. Hippos will travel up to 20 miles (32 km) at night in search of food. Their favorite meal is grass.

Yellow-Billed Stork: The yellow-billed stork migrates annually from Western Europe to Southern Africa. A distance of over 4,000 miles (6,400 km). They do not care to socialize with each other very much and like to live in isolation.

Visit sikulu.com to learn more about these animals. (Be sure to get your parent's permission before visiting Sikulu.com).

Zambia

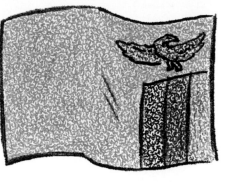

• Zambia is home to about 11 million people. There are more than 72 ethnic groups represented in Zambia each with their own language. However, English is the official language.

• Zambia is a landlocked country that is bordered by the Democratic Republic of Congo to the north, Tanzania to the north east, Malawi to the east, Mozambique, Zimbabwe and Namibia to the south and Angola to the west.

• Zambia is a land of infinite beauty. Almost one third of the country is reserved for national parks and game reserves.

• Zambia is also home to 17 waterfalls including the mighty Victoria Falls or Mosi-ao-Tunya as it is known locally.

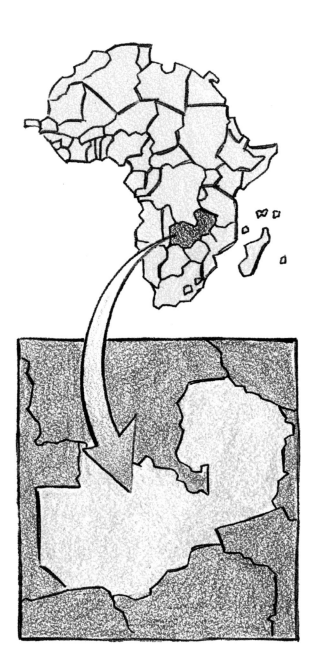

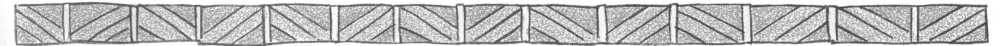

About the Author

Kunle Oguneye was born and raised in Nigeria. He has lived in the United States for the last thirteen years, spending the last four of those years in the Puget Sound Area. He left a career in technology in order to pursue his love for children's story-telling.

This is the first in a series of adventures that follow Sikulu, the spider, and Harambe, the hippo, as they travel to different countries in Africa.